Disclaimer

The medical information provided in this book is of a general nature and cannot substitute for the advice of a doctor, nurse, pharmacist, and/or other medical professionals.

None of the individual writers, contributors, system operators, developers, or sponsors of A Mom and Dad's Guide to Preeclampsia can take any responsibility for the results or consequences of any attempt to use or adopt any of the information presented within the book.

Nothing in A Mom and Dad's Guide to Preeclampsia or MyPreeclampsia.com should construe as an attempt to offer or render a medical opinion or otherwise engage in the practice of medicine.

This book is dedicated to my extraordinary wife, Elizabeth, and our remarkable son, Owen. You both are my greatest inspiration.

Contents

Introduction

Let us begin our journey of discovery with the realization of what preeclampsia is. My intention is not to scare you, but to inform you of what it is and what to look for. It is in knowing what to look for that you can save your own life, the life of your baby, or the life of someone that you love. Preeclampsia is extremely serious and has the potential to be life threatening. It is categorized with other hypertensive disorders, such as eclampsia, HELLP syndrome, toxemia, and Pregnancy Induced Hypertension (PIH). Together, these illnesses account for the leading cause of infant and maternal death. Our hearts go out to the beautiful mommies and babies who aren't with their families today. It breaks my heart to think of the families that are missing a loved one due to preeclampsia. It is this reason that I am committed to helping the mission of the Preeclampsia Foundation. This incredible resource has many dedicated, wonderful people that are helping to create awareness, provide increased education, progress research, support the families who are suffering a loss, and so much more...

What is Preeclampsia?

There are various characteristics which define preeclampsia, including high blood pressure and protein in the mom's urine. If you begin experiencing...:

- Blurred vision or spots in your vision
- Rapid weight gain
- Headaches that appear out of nowhere
- Swelling, especially in your hands, feet, and face

...these are immediate concerns and should be directed toward your doctor. Unfortunately, many women experience very few symptoms and have no idea they are quickly developing preeclampsia. This is why education is so important. It could easily save the life of mom, baby, or, more hopefully, both.

Preeclampsia is a serious condition that develops in approximately 2-8% of all pregnant women, and is more common during a woman's first pregnancy.[1,2] The condition consists of pregnancy-induced high blood pressure and high protein levels in the urine. Other symptoms include swelling (usually in the feet, ankles and legs) and pain in the upper central abdomen.

Preeclampsia can lead to premature births or cause the baby to have a low birth weight. Without treatment, preeclampsia can develop into eclampsia, which is characterized by seizures and can be fatal. High blood pressure disorders during pregnancy, including preeclampsia are the leading causes of pregnancy-related deaths worldwide.[3, 4] This is just one end of the range of problems caused by preeclampsia. It is also the primary reason for premature births, since the only way to end it is for doctors to induce labor.[5] And premature births of course cause a range of health problems for the child, such as low IQ and learning disabilities.[6] The good news is that with a careful diet, preeclampsia can be overcome or even avoided altogether.

Once it is known that you have preeclampsia, it is crucial to find a capable doctor who will provide the best care for you. Don't be afraid to ask your current doctor if they have experience managing the care of a mom-to-be with preeclampsia. You see, if this is a younger doctor, it may be their first preeclampsia pregnancy; you don't want to be their first. Politely ask if there is any other doctor in the practice who is more familiar and better suited to this delicate task.

Once you find the right doctor, do exactly as they say. This doesn't imply that you should follow blindly, so be sure to ask questions and equip yourself with the right tools. Have them explain everything that they instruct you to do as to how that will benefit everyone involved.

It has been said that people resist change. This is not entirely true. What people resist is being changed. People can change if they desire it. This book provides tips and advice for both moms and dads dealing with preeclampsia. This will make an interesting story if it is merely read; however, it may be life changing if a decision is made to act upon the information. There are ideas presented that will not only apply to preeclampsia, but ideas for living life to a more rewarding and fulfilling level.

Each section is geared for both moms and dads who are searching for guidance on preeclampsia. With all the books out there, we could not find any practical information to show us how other people dealt with this syndrome. The only books available were medical journals and books for doctors. Where were the books for regular people who want to know what to expect?

A Mom and Dad's Guide to Preeclampsia has been written to accomplish just that – to be a guidebook. Throughout these chapters, there are helpful tips and principles, along with real life stories that serve to illustrate how my wife and I made it through. We will also share what we would change if we were to go through it again. This is our story and how our lives changed (for the better) in the process.

Some people will choose to focus only on how bad it is and the complications that arise because of it. Other people will focus on how they can remain healthy for as long as possible before having to deliver their baby. This will allow the developing baby all the extra time possible to grow in the safety of the mother's womb. So, while reading this book, think about the decisions that you are currently making and decide if there is anything that you might want to do differently. After all, it is the little things done repeatedly that make the huge changes. Just like the principle behind compound interest, the sooner you start, the richer you will be in life.

What to Look For

This is probably going to be the most important chapter in the entire book. It makes sense, then, to place it at the beginning of the book. The information listed here may just save your life. Since preeclampsia can exist without any symptoms, it is important for pregnant women to get regular checkups by their doctor.

High Blood Pressure

A blood pressure reading above 140/90 followed by another reading above that level six hours later is the first sign of preeclampsia. This is the silent killer. You can't feel, smell, see, hear, or taste high blood pressure. "What is considered high blood pressure?" That is a great question, and truthfully, it is different for everyone. This is why it is important to know what your baseline blood pressure is. Your baseline blood pressure is your normal reading while resting, preferably before preeclampsia or even pregnancy. As a general rule, 140/90 is considered high. Many women have blood pressure that is dangerously below that. For this reason, the National Institutes of Health caution that any rise of 30 mm Hg systolic (upper number) and 15 mm Hg diastolic (lower number) warrant closer observation. If you have an increase of 5 or 10 in any number, top or bottom, don't even risk it; tell your doctor as soon as possible. It is so much better to be safe than sorry with this one. Because blood pressure readings are such an integral part of monitoring preeclampsia, we have developed a free printable sheet to make noticing trends easier. The free printable Log Book is available on http://MyPreeclampsia.com.

Aches and Pains

The other symptom that can be noticed is pain in the upper central abdomen (above the stomach but below the breasts). Often women mistake this pain for heartburn, which is common during pregnancy. However, this abdominal pain has some differences; it does not radiate up the esophagus into the throat and mouth, it is not reduced by antacids and it can be extremely severe, sometimes described as the worst pain ever felt. If back pain is from preeclampsia, it could possibly be the liver that is in trouble. Tell your doctor immediately about your back pain and the exact location of the pain, even if you don't think it could be related. For instance, the pain may be in your right shoulder or even stomach. My Liz would have stomach pains that felt to her like heart burn, and so she would eat antacid tablets. She didn't know that it was a symptom of preeclampsia. Now, hopefully, you won't make her same mistake and let it go unmentioned.

Headaches can act as a painful realization that something may not be right. My lovely wife would get some killer migraines that would put her into bed. Even then, she would sometimes wake up with the same headache. She would try her best not to take any pain medicine, but sometimes, she had no choice. Her doctor told her to take a Tylenol and to make sure to stay away from aspirin. Before taking any over the counter medications, obviously, ask your doctor first. And, while you're asking your doctor, please notify them of the headaches as well. Tell them the severity and see what they say regarding when it should become a concern.

Rapid Weight Gain

Other symptoms include sudden weight gain, ringing in the ears and headaches, dizziness or fainting. Preeclampsia is a serious condition that every pregnant woman should be on the lookout for. All pregnant ladies gain a few extra baby pounds. The difference with preeclampsia is that the weight gain is more than 2 lbs. in a week or 6 in a month. There is nothing that can be done about the extra weight, and the good news is that it is mostly fluid. Therefore, easy come, easy go (after the delivery that is). While pregnant, never try dieting or weight loss supplements no matter how natural they claim to be. The best thing to do is eat healthy foods while staying away from salt and artificial sweeteners. Your doctor should be noticing if you have increased weight gain, since they measure you at every checkup. However, still keep your own records in case they fail to see the upward trend. Don't assume that they must know about it. Bring it up, and discuss it with them.

We have a chapter on Proper Eating along with recipes towards the end of the book. While these in no way will cure your preeclampsia, it will still be vital in staying as healthy as possible. This is, of course, important for nourishing a developing baby as well as preparing for the trauma that the mommy's body will suffer after the pregnancy and the healing that will take place.

To facilitate faster healing and to provide the best start for your child, really commit yourself to living a healthy lifestyle. This includes taking prenatal vitamins. An excellent vitamin that we found was the Pharmanex LifePak PreNatal. We truly believe in the high quality product that they consistently deliver. They have many leading scientists, like the father of antioxidants, Dr. Lester Packer , behind their company and products. Also, in his the book, *Where Have All the Leaders Gone*, Lee Iacocca talks about why more companies should be like Pharmanex and how they provide so much good in the world (partly by feeding over 189,000,000 meals to children since 2002). While vitamins are recommended throughout pregnancy, there are also things to avoid to keep everyone healthy. Things like smoking, drinking, medications (legal and illegal, unless prescribed by your doctor), caffeine, and sweeteners (both natural and artificial) should all be avoided. Make sure to drink lots and lots and lots of water; filtered is best. There are many contaminants in tap water and well water that should be filtered out.

Zig Ziglar once asked the question, "How many of y'all own a million dollar race horse? If you did own a million dollar race horse, would ya let him stay up half the night drinking coffee and booze, smoking cigarettes, and eating junk food? And if ya did, how many races would he win?" We can all probably agree that he wouldn't win many. Now, would you treat a $10 dog like that? How about a $5 cat? What about a billion dollar body? We all need to start treating our bodies like they're worth a billion dollars; because they are! This is the only body you've got, and it needs to be in the best condition possible to house the most precious gift in the world: a billion dollar baby.

Body Swelling

Symptoms that a woman can be on the lookout for herself is swelling of the hands, feet, and sometimes face. It is often called pitting edema because when the skin on the affected area is pushed in, the indentation, or "pit" does not bounce back immediately, but takes a few seconds to disappear. All pregnant ladies will gain weight and likely swell a bit. There is a huge difference, however, between a little weight gain and swelling and edema. Edema is when your body stores excess fluid, and your hands, feet, and/or face will become more swollen. This can also have an effect on your vision as the swelling can place pressure on your eyeballs, causing some women to experience seeing spots or blurred vision. Liz, for instance, would see stars for brief periods; like when you stand up too fast or you clench your eyes closed really hard.

Sometimes, when we gain or lose weight, it is hard to see it on ourselves because the change in subtle over the course of days and weeks. Ask your friends or relatives who may not see you every single day if you appear swollen in your hands, face, or feet. If you have a before pregnancy picture of yourself, try looking at that to compare. Liz had so much swelling in her feet that she could no longer wear her shoes. She had so much swelling in her hands that it actually caused her pain, especially while trying to sleep. She would complain of a pins-and-needles feeling in her hands, and I felt helpless to take the pain away. In my chapter Tips for

Sleeping, I recommend a few ideas to help with sleeping and to better manage the pain associated with swollen hands. The bottom line, tell your doctor about any swelling that you notice.

Protein in Your Urine

Another is a protein level in the pregnant women's urine of 300 mg or more. This is another very serious condition that may also rank right up there with high blood pressure. Proteinuria, or protein in your urine, is caused by your kidneys becoming damaged and "spilling" protein from your blood into your urine. Because the blood vessels in your kidneys become damaged, your urine may become darker than usual. Your doctor should be taking urine samples from you at every checkup to monitor protein levels. If it looks like there may be excess protein in your pee (a tiny bit is normal), then your doctor will most likely make you perform a 24 hour urine collection. This is where your store your peepee in the fridge for 24 hrs without missing a single drop. You then take this urine to the lab, and they send the results back to your doctor. I go over this in much more detail in a later chapter, The Joy of Peeing. If your urine is dark, it may simply mean that you need more water intake and that you are dehydrated. If after drinking plenty of water your urine is still dark, make sure that your doctor is aware of the situation.

Throwing Up

Nausea is a terrible feeling and could be a symptom of preeclampsia. While most pregnant ladies deal with nausea to some extent, it is still important to mention to your doctor.

Have them test your urine and your blood pressure to ensure that you are not developing preeclampsia or another hypertensive disorder. It just isn't worth risking.

Eyes Playing Tricks

If your eyes begin to play tricks on you, call your doctor immediately, or just go straight to the hospital. These tricks are usually temporary, meaning they will come and go. Don't wait for it to happen again and again; go and get checked out. The risk is far too great to let it go. If you begin seeing spots, things get blurry, lights seem to flash, you lose sight completely for a moment, it looks like lights have halos around them (like when you swim in the swimming pool too long), or your eyes become very sensitive to the light, see your doctor immediately.

Anxious, Nervous, Confused?

These could all indicate an increase in blood pressure by forcing your heart to work harder to pump blood. If you feel like your heart is racing or you are anxious or confused, please go and get yourself checked by your doctor.

Abrupt Reflexes

Do you remember when you used to get your school physical, and they would tap your knee in just the right spot to make it jump? Well, it should jump just a little. If you or your husband/boyfriend tap your knee and it jerks up harder than usual, this could be of concern. Tell your doctor and have them tap your knee to see if it is something serious, like preeclampsia.

Like I said before, education is the key to surviving

preeclampsia. Simply knowing what to look for can save your life! It is that vitally important to know what to look for, know the symptoms, and protect yourself. Never leave it up to the doctor. You need to start taking responsibility and pay close attention to your changing body. Ask your husband or boyfriend for help. Make sure that he knows what to look for also. Sometimes, someone of the "outside" can see things that maybe you might miss. Or he can nudge you a bit to call the doctor or go to the hospital. The mommy may be thinking about the headache at hand or the nausea in the present, and she may completely miss the symptoms that have been building. Again, if you have or think you may have any of the symptoms or condition listed above, please for the love of yourself and your unborn baby, get checked out. It is so much better to play it safe. Better an inconvenient car ride and ER visit than the alternative.

* * *

You may have noticed now that I have mentioned seeing your doctor *immediately*, in most cases, for many symptoms and conditions. I have also mentioned calling your doctor immediately regarding many symptoms and conditions. It is like the old story of the preacher who recently moved to a new parish. The first week he gave his sermon, it was a great sermon that taught a couple very valuable lessons and the congregation enjoyed it. The next week, he gave the exact same sermon. The week after that, he again delivered the same sermon. By the 4th time of delivering the same message, some elders of the church took the preacher aside and mentioned that he was pretty much giving the exact same sermon week after week. The preacher looked at them and smiled and said, "I'm glad you noticed. And I will keep giving the same sermon until people start taking action on the words that I am saying." Please take action, call your doctor immediately if you experience any of the above symptoms or if you just don't feel right. If something feels "off" or "wrong" and it's after hours, go straight to the ER. We love all of the pregnant ladies out there and wish everyone a safe and happy pregnancy.

Blood Pressure

A characteristic of preeclampsia is high blood pressure. Since there will be a need to have countless blood pressure readings taken, it makes sense to buy a quality blood pressure monitor. We suggest purchasing a mid-range device for $50 that will provide fairly accurate results. The reason we say "fairly accurate" is because every time a mommy's blood pressure is taken, the results will vary. This is why it is important to note the average of 3 readings every time.

Our doctor instructed us to record Liz's blood pressure 3 to 4 times per day. At first, this seems easy enough. Every few hours, grab the blood pressure monitor, take the average of 3 readings, and record it in our journal. The reality of these constant readings is that we began having numbers written everywhere. We used the backs of envelopes, old receipts, and scrap pieces of paper lying around. You name it, and we used it! The problem with this method is keeping track of our readings and being able to see trends. After a month or so, we finally began using a small journal to keep it all in one place.

Now, it was about this time that my grandmother, Gramma-Margie, informed us of a little trick that she uses when going to her doctor to have her blood pressure taken. The trick is to wiggle your toes as your blood pressure is being measured. Whether or not toe wiggling would merely distract the mind of the person getting their blood pressure taken or if it would actually alter the person's physical blood pressure through movement of the limbs was unknown to us. What is known is that you do not want inaccurate results. If you know of any other "tricks", DO NOT use them. There is a very real danger if your blood pressure gets too high for too long. Ask your doctor what those magic numbers are for your particular situation, because everyone runs at a different pressure.

Start a Journal

Our tips for the constant blood pressure monitoring would be to start a journal or log book to keep organized track of the hundreds of future readings. Make sure to record the date and time of each reading, along with the average blood pressure result (average of 3). We actually developed a printable journal page that you can download for free on our website, MyPreeclampsia.com, and then find yourself a really sweet folder for the printouts.

Think Happy Thoughts

When we would take Liz's blood pressure, we made sure to both think happy thoughts of low numbers, and thank God for His goodness in making sure that our baby was born healthy and whole. Her blood pressure was always high, but we managed to keep it just low enough to continue our little man developing for a solid 8 months.

Relax

The devoted man's role in the blood pressure process can be to get the device ready for use. This includes plugging it in and placing the cuff on your beautiful wife or girlfriend's arm. Before pressing the start button, remind everyone to remain calm and relaxed, thinking those good thoughts. Then when the number is displayed, press start 2 more times and recording the average of those 3 readings. I would even take my blood pressure just for fun and to make sure that the device was functioning properly. Experiment with different rooms in the house as some rooms may have more feng shui. Always try to take her blood pressure lying down, because this should give more accurate results as well. We also waited roughly 5 minutes after lying down to give her body a chance to rest after walking to the bed and before slapping the blood pressure cuff on her arm.

Eat More Garlic

A great way we kept her blood pressure in control was by eating ultra healthy foods. One in particular is garlic. According to Dr. Sooranna, Dr. Das, and Ms. Hirani from the UK, garlic can cut the risk of preeclampsia in pregnant women and may also boost the birth weight of babies who are on their way to being born too small. We had not heard about this research at the time, but we did eat a fair amount of garlic to help regulate her high blood pressure.

Not only garlic is a great food to keep in the house at all times, but also just about every vegetable and fruit is fantastic to eat on a daily basis. If local organic fruits and vegetables are available, please spend the extra few dollars to buy those. Organics are much healthier, and truthfully, what is more important than the health of your baby? Every time that I would go shopping, each item had to undergo strict dietary and nutritional guidelines before making it into our cart. Public enemy #1, beside artificial sweeteners, is sodium. Sodium is a huge contributor to high blood pressure, even without the addition of preeclampsia. This single ingredient is probably the hardest one to filter out of our diets. This is because sodium is in everything! Any packaged food and drink is guaranteed to have sodium. That is why it is so important to buy and eat fruits and vegetables instead of processed or manufactured foods, like chips and soft drinks. If you have to have chips and drinks other than water, choose organic chips and drinks, because they can be healthier. Be careful to eat these in moderation. They are still horrible substitutes for the real deal. After browsing your supermarket shelves, you may notice that limiting the sodium intake will actually eliminate nearly all frozen foods and most packaged items. This is good! You want to stay away from these as much as possible while pregnant.

If it has not yet been discovered, the man here is going to be doing nearly all of the shopping, cooking, and cleaning. If your wife or girlfriend is placed on bed rest, that means she is to stay in bed, except for going to the bathroom. This may sound daunting at first, but after a habit is made of shopping, cooking, and cleaning, it really takes no additional effort, just willingness. By having the will to do it, anything can be accomplished.

Proper Eating

There is no known cure for preeclampsia, but some measures can be taken to reduce the risks. A healthy diet containing the proper amounts of protein, vitamins, minerals and other nutrients can go a long way to minimizing a woman's chances of developing this potentially fatal condition. That's why the food mommies put into their body is so important! Not only in pregnancy are the right foods important, but especially with preeclampsia, where there is extra protein in the urine and very high blood pressure. As with all diets and eating plans, discuss all changes with your doctor first. They can help you with good choices as to which foods are appropriate and which to avoid at all costs. Also, if we recommend a food that causes allergies, please do not eat it. For instance, almonds are really healthy, but not if you are allergic to them!

Fiber

Fiber is one of those things that is helpful in a pregnant woman's diet due to the increased risk of developing hemorrhoids during pregnancy. One study found that women with a high fiber intake had a 51% lower chance of developing preeclampsia.[7] Another larger study confirmed this finding.[8]

Protein

It is a well-known fact that excess protein in the pregnant woman's urine is one of the symptoms of preeclampsia. The quick conclusion that might be drawn is that a pregnant woman that is eating too much protein is at a higher risk of developing preeclampsia. But actually, the exact opposite is true. When a woman is not getting enough protein in her diet, her body will start to break down her own body tissue in order to get the amount of protein needed to keep her baby healthy. A result of this breakdown is that there will be an excessive amount of protein in the woman's urine.

The few studies that were done on protein intake have failed to prove that a protein deficiency can cause preeclampsia or that additional protein can prevent preeclampsia. But many of these studies weren't well designed, so to be on the safe side aim to get 80 to 100 grams of protein every day. To put that into easy-to-understand measures, here is an example of protein from typical meals and snacks.

Food	Grams of Protein
A steak	32
A chicken breast	24
A fish filet	22
An egg	8
A stick of string cheese	8
Total protein for the day	94

Good sources of protein are:

- Lean beef
- Skinless chicken breast
- Lean pork
- Turkey breast
- Whey protein
- Nuts and nut oils
- Seeds
- Fat-free, low fat or organic milk and dairy products
- Organic eggs
- Wild salmon
- Wheat germ

Fats

Several studies have provided evidence that a high fat intake may increase the risk of developing preeclampsia.[9-14] Therefore it is best to avoid fatty foods, like fatty meats, fried foods and oily recipes. Instead try baking, grilling, boiling and steaming foods. Also, a high intake of the healthy omega-3 fats seems to reduce the risk of developing preeclampsia, though one study found that getting too much cod liver oil may be more harmful than helpful.[15-23] So eat foods rich in omega-3s like:

- Salmon
- Sardines
- Mackerel
- Herring

- Anchovies
- Caviar
- Flaxseeds
- Walnuts
- Spinach

Food is not the only way to get your omega-3s, especially since pregnant women can be picky eaters! Another good way to ensure you get enough omega-3s is to take a daily fish oil or omega-3 supplement. Most are capsules, which are easier for pregnant women to swallow.

Calcium

Calcium is the nutrient with the best study results showing that it reduces the risk of preeclampsia. A study of approximately 15,000 women performed by The University of the Witwatersrand and the University of Fort Hare in South Africa found that women who took 1000 mg of calcium daily during pregnancy were half as likely to develop preeclampsia than those receiving a placebo.[24] Foods rich in calcium include spinach, milk, cheese and yogurt. Of course, you can also get your calcium from a supplement. In a study, women who took a calcium supplement were far less likely to develop preeclampsia.[25]

Salt

Interestingly, studies have shown that salt has no impact on preeclampsia, and researchers have even suggested that a salt restriction is not recommended during pregnancy.[26-29] This of course doesn't mean to eat all the salty junk foods you can find, but instead means not to eat only unsalted foods. One good health tip for all people though is to replace regular table salt with sea salt or Himalayan crystal salt, since they are healthier types of salt.

Vitamins

There are certain vitamins that are important in preventing or getting rid of preeclampsia. First is vitamin C, which is a strong antioxidant. Studies have shown that in women with preeclampsia, their blood vitamin C levels are low.[30-34] No studies have demonstrated that vitamin C prevents preeclampsia though.

Next is vitamin E—another antioxidant vitamin. Like vitamin C, no studies have shown that vitamin E alone can prevent preeclampsia, though studies show that it is also at low levels in women with preeclampsia.[35-38] A study was done where 283 women were given either 1000 mg/day vitamin C and 400 IU/day of vitamin E or a placebo. The women taking the vitamin C and vitamin E supplements showed 22% less cases of preeclampsia.[39] Other studies have been done that are not as conclusive about the positive effects of these vitamins.

But since vitamin C and E are antioxidant vitamins that work against some of the root causes of preeclampsia, they are highly recommended.

Low levels of vitamin A and beta-carotene (a form of vitamin A) have been found in women with preeclampsia.[40-43] It is not known if it is a cause of preeclampsia or just a symptom. Since high levels of vitamin A are potentially harmful for a fetus, only extra beta-carotene supplements should be taken. And foods with vitamin A can also be eaten, such as sweet potatoes, carrots, mangoes, spinach, cantaloupe, apricots and eggs.

Folic acid, a common B vitamin in pre-natal vitamins, is also a potential help for preventing preeclampsia as shown in studies.[44-46] Many cereals, tortillas and breads are fortified with folic acid, plus it is in whole grain products, lentils, peas and some green vegetables.

Vitamin D supplementation was shown in a study to reduce the risk of developing preeclampsia by 27%.[47] Vitamin D is obtained from direct exposure of the skin to the sun and by taking vitamin D supplements.

Magnesium

A study showed that women who took a magnesium supplement had a 52% lower occurrence of seizures due to eclampsia.[48] Another previous study observed that taking magnesium supplements lowers the risk of developing preeclampsia.[49]

Zinc

Women with a low zinc level are more likely to develop preeclampsia during pregnancy.[50]

Getting Enough of These Nutrients

While it would be great to eat a diet that provides enough of all these nutrients, that is not possible every day. So it is best to take a few supplements to ensure you are getting everything you need to help protect you against preeclampsia.

Recommended supplements are:

1. A pre-natal multivitamin containing vitamins C, E, folic acid, calcium, magnesium, zinc and vitamin D.

2. A fish oil or omega-3 supplement (not necessary if your pre-natal contains DHA).

3. A fiber supplement like Metamucil.

Other Steps to Take

There are other things you can do to keep yourself healthy in order to prevent or reduce preeclampsia. These are not proven as helping in any way, but are known to improve general health.

- Drink at least eight 8 oz glasses of filtered water every day.
- Avoid caffeine, alcohol and smoking.
- Take Epsom salts baths, making sure the water is warm not hot.

For everyone's convenience we have included a complete 30-Day Meal Plan that's not only easy to follow, it's also delicious! For ease of reference, we placed the Meal Plan at the end of the book.

Clothes Buying

To add a certain degree of validity to this section regarding maternity wear and pregnancy clothes, my amazing wife, Liz, has guided this author.

Liz warns, do not go overboard and buy a ton of clothes. The key is to find enough maternity wear to get you through the preeclampsia weight gain without ending up with a whole new wardrobe of pregnancy clothes. Also get 1 or 2 new "skinny" clothes to focus on the future and your "pre-baby" post-baby weight goals. Since so much of the weight is water weight and retained fluids when you have preeclampsia, after delivery, the weight falls off fast. Within the first 24 hours after giving birth, Liz had peepee'd 26 lbs, plus the 4 lbs, 11 oz of our spectacular baby, Owen, for a net loss of over 30 lbs!

Liz swears by the H&M store in malls. If you are fortunate enough to have one nearby, you are in the lucky minority. She used to shop at H&M all the time when she lived in Washington D.C., but since moving back to Orlando, she left the store and its bargains behind. It was not until just recently did H&M decide to grace Orlando with its presence in the Florida mall. If shopping and there are not many options, which is how it was for us, try a local Target or Wal-Mart. Both of these stores are great for maternity wear, and have really awesome deals on clothes.

The way for daddies to help with the clothes buying experience is by going with their amazing ladies to a few different stores. You will both be getting climate-controlled exercise and will be spending quality time together. Not to worry, guys, your pregnant companions can only shop for so long with swollen feet, nausea, and constant peeing. This is especially true if you are in the collecting urine phase of preeclampsia.

Dads can also get into the shopping when it is partially for them. Maybe someone needs a few new pairs of boxers or socks. It may not be glamorous, like videogames; however, sometimes, the basics are needed and neglected. If you happen to find yourself in a Target, there is a videogame section. Maybe your powers of persuasion can convince your better half a new videogame is a necessity?

A super benefit to shopping with your special lady will be to push the shopping cart with her purse and goodies in it. This will allow your awesome mom-to-be access to both her hands for lightning fast riffling through clothes. And without having to navigate the cart, they can zip through aisles and racks like nobody's business! Your beautiful mommy will find what she is looking for in no time. She will also greatly appreciate your help during the entire shopping experience.

Lastly, please be careful not to judge or make note of how much she is spending on maternity clothes. She should already be aware of the family's monetary situation. Chances are, she knows the state of affairs and does not need to be reminded all the time. Of course, if it starts getting out of hand, speak up. Otherwise, let her spend a few extra dollars. The feeling that she will get from having new clothes to wear and going shopping with her man will be extremely beneficial to her immune system and body as a whole.

The Joy of Peeing

The P in Preeclampsia stands for Peeing. The doctors need to constantly measure the amount of protein in the urine. For this purpose, they have designed an ingenious contraption known as the Hat. You may or may not already know about the Hat, depending on how far along in the pregnancy you are. For those of you who do not know, the Hat is a little plastic cup that roughly resembles an upside-down cowboy hat. The brim is what rests between the toilet seat and bowl and basically supports the cup that women pee into. If you are currently uncomfortable walking around with pee in your hands, not to worry, it will soon pass. It may sound like this section is going to be geared for the ladies. After all, they are the ones who will be doing the peeing. Guess again, dads. You can still be a huge help to your pregnant mommy.

The object of collecting and storing (did we forget to mention you will be storing your pee?) your urine is to continually monitor your protein levels. Your kidneys are spilling protein into your pee and are essentially failing. If your kidneys are releasing too much protein too quickly, then they will have to deliver your baby to save the lives of both mother and child. That is why collecting and storing the pee is so important and such a necessity when dealing with preeclampsia.

How to Collect Pee

The steps of collecting the urine are pretty self-explanatory. Urinate into the Hat every time you go to the bathroom. Take that urine very carefully, so as not to spill, over to the large jug given to you along with your Hat. After pouring the contents of your Hat into your jug, place the cap on the jug and rest the jug ever-so-neatly in your refrigerator.

Obviously, the mom needs to pee in her own Hat. There is not much that the dad can do to help with this action. What the dad can do is keep an eye on the toilet and on his pregnant lady. If he notices that, on occasion, she forgets to pour the Hat into the jug, go ahead and do it for her. Do not tell her about it; just do it. If you think a little pee is too gross to touch, you may not be ready for parenthood. Better yet, instead of dads noticing that our awesome ladies forgot to bring her Hat to the jug, bring the jug to her. Another idea is to open the fridge and unscrew the cap as she is coming back from the bathroom. This way all she has to do is pour it in and place her Hat back on the toilet. The whole operation runs much more smoothly this way.

Some tips that we suggest detail the placement of the pee in the fridge. Believe me; you do not want your lady's 100-degree pee next to your milk or juices. You also do not want it next to your deli meats or cheeses. In fact, you probably do not want it next to anything that you plan on eating. The pee, of course, is in a jug with a cap on it, but the thought and sight of it resting against your food items can be enough to turn you off from eating them. For these reasons, we chose to store her peepee in the door of our refrigerator and even gave it its very own shelf. If you or your lady's pouring skills are hit and miss from the Hat to the jug, you may want to consider placing a small towel on the shelf underneath the jug to catch any stray drops.

If both mom and dad have not already noticed, there will be a LOT of peeing happening on a daily basis. My wife, Liz, actually went so often that we had to begin requesting additional jugs every time we went in to drop off our collection. Do not be afraid to ask for more jugs. The first time it happened, we used an empty milk jug. After we began asking for 1 extra, they started giving us 3 jugs, just in case. We did not see any additional charges on our bill for the extra 2 jugs either, so go ahead and ask for them early on. It may just save you an embarrassing milk jug incident.

Kids

If you already have kids, make sure to involve them every step of the way, while their precious mommy is pregnant with preeclampsia. The best part is that your children (or child) will want to help. Not only will they feel really wonderful knowing that they are helping mommy and daddy, it will also keep the family together and interacting. Tony Robbins points out that people operate in the interest of others. When people (and kids) become emotionally charged, they can and will do anything. Get them to understand that mommy is sick and that you need their help to make her feel better. If either of you have had a cold, you know that they want to help bring you things like soup and sandwiches and drinks. This should be no different – only longer.

Kids are great at small chores, like setting the table. Let them know what great jobs they are doing and help them feel important in the house. After all, they are contributing towards a greater good, which is welcoming home a new brother or sister to love. Depending on how old they are, they may not be ready to put knives on the table, but the napkins, forks, and spoons should be acceptable. I know my wife, Liz, often times did not feel up to eating at the dinner table. Instead, we would set the coffee table in front of the TV and eat on the couch. Or, we would all eat in bed! If you decide to have a picnic in bed, plan on extra napkins, as accidents tend to happen. We would even lay down a towel under our food to expect the inevitable spill.

There are tons of other little things around the house that they can help with. For instance, washing the fruits and vegetables for snacks and dinner is an easy task for almost any age child.

Another idea for keeping kids entertained while their mom deals with her preeclampsia is by having an arts and crafts session. The way it will differ from their usual arts and crafts is by having them make special cards for mommy. They could also make homemade jewelry for mom to wear because she is so gorgeous.

Send kids outside to pick pretty wildflowers for a custom flower arrangement. Then tie a ribbon around the bunch and present them to mommy.

Try to make games out of everything. For example, if your child can get their own beverages, see how quickly they can get mom more water, and time how long it takes. Or see how high they can fill your glass with water without spilling any. Even if they do spill some, who cares. Its just water! Make little things fun and exciting as much as possible.

Sometimes kids just gotta play! See if they can entertain themselves for a couple of hours, since mommies with preeclampsia need extra sleep. Better yet, see if grandma and grandpa can watch junior for the afternoon. Your kids may even like a slumber party at grandma and grandpa's house! I know I did when I was a kid. If all else fails, perhaps they can go over to a friend's house to play. This way, there is parental supervision, and your child gets to interact with another person his or her own age. Playing by himself or herself or merely sitting in front of a TV or computer may get boring after awhile.

There are so many things that kids can do to help their mom (and dad) with her preeclampsia. The key is to try and keep them involved so that they are not feeling left out or ignored. If you are giving your kids attention and showing them how much you love them and that they are helping a tremendous amount, it should prevent them from doing bad things to get attention. That is all kids want, really – to know you love them very much and to give them lots of attention. Whether it is positive or negative, they want your attention. Make sure that your attention is positive by giving them positive interaction. Every once in a while, they may even get a new toy or ice cream to show how excellent a job they are doing at caring for mommy.

Laugh Often

Never take your preeclampsia too seriously. Be smart about it, listen to your doctors, and do exactly what they tell you to do. However, let them look after the preeclampsia. Mom and dad need to focus on the positive, seeing their beautiful baby coming into this world perfect and healthy.

I once heard Dr. Deepak Chopra, say that if we are laughing and feeling exhilarated and joyous, that our bodies will produce powerful anti-cancer drugs, like interleukin and interferon. Why not produce hundreds of thousands of dollars of free interleukin and interferon by laughing whole-heartedly as often as possible!

After a hearty laugh, bodies and hearts feel happy. It is a wonderful way to go through life, regardless of preeclampsia or not. Some tips for laughing frequently include watching TV shows and movies that you both consider funny. Hilarious is actually best, so strive to watch hilarious programs. The more laughing that everyone is doing, the better for everyone: mom, dad, and baby.

We personally love to watch America's Funniest Videos (AFV), and we both laugh constantly! That show might not be for everyone, as it is a bit slapstick, but surely, there is a program that always manages to tickle your funny bone!

Speaking of tickling your funny bone, get into tickle fights with each other as often as possible! We highly recommend at least 1 per day if your doctor allows it and you have the stamina. In fact, try to have the tickle fights early on in the pregnancy/preeclampsia, because later, you may end up on bed rest, at which point tickle fights will have to be put on hold until after the baby is delivered.

Romance

Keep those fires lit, people! Preeclampsia can be very trying on a relationship when the mommy is forced to be on bed rest. This leaves the lion's share of things to do around the house resting on the daddy. It can sometimes become overwhelming, but with the right attitude and emotions, anything can be achieved. These are some suggestions for keeping the fires lit after the bun is in the oven.

A great way to be romantic during these trying times is by taking a few minutes to light some candles before dinner at least once per week. If you have lights on a dimmer switch, dim all the lights in the house. Light extra candles to create that calming flicker effect. Pour some juice into a wine glass, and recreate the experience of drinking wine.

Liz and I would have fun and not take ourselves too seriously. Sometimes, we would role-play, pretending to be strangers just meeting for the first time. It gave us a chance to get dressed up in an outfit that we would never normally wear. We would also come up with a new name and persona to really try and become a different person.

Another way to be romantic is by picking flowers from outside and leaving them next to her side of the bed. Better yet, if you arise in the morning before your beautiful mommy-to-be, pick the flowers and place them so that she notices them first thing when she wakes up. This way, when she wakes up in the morning, she will arise to the smell of fresh flowers and a colorful bouquet.

We, unfortunately, did not have any extra money to spend on flowers. What we did have, on the other hand, was a neighborhood filled with flowering bushes. If you do not have any flowers outside your own house, borrow a couple from your neighbors or neighborhood in general. Buying bouquets, while beautiful, can really add up. Keep it free, and remember, it really is the thought that counts.

Do not forget to tell your incredible wife or girlfriend how gorgeous she is. Be sincere and compliment her on something specific. A generalized statement like "you look pretty" is nice, but a genuine compliment about how pretty her hair looks or the beautiful color of her eyes will be received much better. I am not saying to make stuff up or just blow hot wind out of your mouth. Be genuine, be sincere, and compliment your hot momma from the heart.

I would try to let my wifey know as often as possible how much I loved her and what a great job she was doing. I would also notice that the color of her eyes would, on occasion, be a stunning emerald green with hazel tones. I would comment on how beautiful her eyes were that day, and I meant it. She would get so excited, and it was easy to see it made her feel good to hear nice things like that.

The next step to romance is to rub those feet! Poor pregnant ladies get swollen feet as it is. Preeclampsia only adds to the swelling. To combat this growing dilemma, take lotion every night, and rub each foot, if only for a few minutes each.

I remember my wife's heels would get so chapped and cracked from her feet being swollen. Because of her swollen feet, she wore sandals most of the time. This seemed to only add to the cracking of her heels. She would appreciate her foot rubs so much! What made it even more special was that she could not reach her own feet, so to have someone else rub her feet for her was delightful. As a tip: when giving foot rubs, try and do it in bed if you have wood floors. We had African teakwood floors in our condo that would show every cute little footprint that she made after getting her foot rub. We had hundreds of little footprints all over the house. The prints were mainly from the couch to the bathroom and from the bed to the bathroom. So, if she is already in bed when the foot rubs commence, it may eliminate the additional prints around the living room.

By this point, you may be asking when I will be getting to the "romance tips". So far, all we have gone over are lighting candles at dinner, flowers by the bed, foot rubs… are you getting the picture yet? To create romance, dads need to become romantic. Help your mom-to-be feel pretty. Create romantic atmospheres and moments that show romantic gestures. Become a kid again, and think of all the small ways to say I love you.

Coping with Numbness

The worst part about the preeclampsia, according to Liz, is the numbness, which leads to pins and needles. Nowhere did this affect her more than in her hands and wrists. When her body began retaining so much water so quickly, she began to experience poor circulation in her extremities.

Liz recommends consistent stretching throughout the entire pregnancy. This is one area that she has decided to focus on more for the next pregnancy. We bought a pregnancy yoga DVD that was a great video and showcased some excellent stretches that are safe and easy enough to do with a baby-belly. Our living arrangements, however, were not ideal for trying to practice yoga while pregnant. We really did not have much room to speak of to stretch out in front of a TV or computer to watch and practice the stretches. Couple that with hard wood floors throughout the house, and it really did not make for a comfortable experience. If you also have hard tile or wood floors, buy 2 squishy yoga mats and stack them together to provide some extra cushion for stretching.

Stinging hands are a sure-fire way to stay up at night. While this problem is more difficult to control, we found some success with soft wrist guards while sleeping. The key is to find ones that keeps the hand and wrist in a straight, natural position to prevent additional pinching of veins and nerves. Also, try to avoid shaking your hands to regain feeling. We learned to avoid this after some friends of ours told us that shaking her hands was making the problem of pins and needles worse. This is because of the pinching of nerves in the wrists, versus the loss of blood flow. Shaking of the hands will usually only add to the discomfort already being experienced.

A good way of taking your amazing pregnant mommy's mind off of her hands would be to offer a nice long backrub. Get out the lotion and go to work on all the different sections of her back. Focus on each area for a few minutes to really provide a quality backrub that should hopefully help her forget about her hands. Even better still, do not stop with her back. Work down to her arms, forearms, and hands to really help stimulate blood flow and promote increased circulation.

Tips for Sleeping

Sleep is a crucial component of any person's health and sanity. The problem with preeclampsia and sleeping for many ladies is the uncomfortable environment surrounding them. There are many reasons a sleeping beauty will wake up throughout the night. Below are some common problems and how to overcome them to get a restful night's sleep.

The first problem is the constant getting up to pee, multiple times, throughout the night. While the dad is not able to pee for mommy, he can help make it easier and more convenient. One way to accomplish this will be to have her sleep on the side of the bed closest to the bathroom. Also, dads need to keep the toilet seat down at all times, without fail.

I personally would rather sit down on the toilet in my own house anyway, so this was never really a problem for us. The biggest obstacle was remembering to remove her Hat in the toilet before using it. If you have 2+ bathrooms in the house, consider using the guest bathroom more often.

A fantastic invention for making nighttime bathroom visits easier is the glowing nightlight. We placed one in our bathroom, and it made it so much nicer to not have to turn on a bright, harsh light and ruin your night vision. Beware not to get a nightlight that is too bright, however, as this may still hurt your eyes.

Another problem that affects sleep quality is the overall temperature of the house. Depending on the time of year and your geographic location, this may not be as difficult to maintain, or as expensive. It seems that pregnant ladies tend to run a degree or 2 warmer than usual because of the 2 heartbeats and all that creation happening inside, so a cooler house should make it easier to sleep.

Our house stayed at a brisk 68 at night and 73 during the day. Living down in Orlando, Florida, during the summer months meant the A/C was running nearly around the clock. The electric company and our mommy really appreciated the cold house though. And sleep is more important than a high electric bill. A tip for the dads out there might be to invest in some long sleeve pajamas to help brave the Siberian winters that are soon to be felt.

Lastly, a really wonderful invention that Liz swears by is the Back Max Body Wedge pillow. The problem was when she was flat on her back she would become nauseous. If she was too upright, using pillows stuffed behind her head, she could not sleep either. The solution was the Back Max pillow that kept her in a comfortable reclined position. It reminds me of a Craftmatic® adjustable bed, like in the hospital. Only it can be used in the bed or on the couch. It helps to relieve pressure points while lying down, and it is actually considered an orthopedic wedge. We did not purchase the pillowcase for it, nor did we feel it was necessary. She never ended up spilling anything on it, and she used it everyday, often while eating in bed. If you generally spill things, you might consider getting the pillowcase, but like I said, we did not get it, saved a few dollars in the process, and never missed it once.

No Questions Asked Money

Jim Rohn taught me this invaluable philosophy of no questions asked money. It was discovered out of the realization that asking for money is uncomfortable and a bit degrading. Just because the mom may not be working, does not imply that she is not contributing to the household. After all, she is caring for the most precious cargo ever created! She should be compensated, generously, for her ultimate sacrifice. As soon as I learned of this principal, I took action.

A week later, I opened my lovely wife a no questions asked account that was for her personal spending. Now, we did not have a lot of money. We actually were quite poor. Lucky for us (and especially her) to start this account does not take a fortune. Just a few dollars a week can be enough to fund it. The idea being I keep filling it up, and she gets to spend the money on anything she desires. She no longer needs to ask permission to buy something; she can just get it. A rule of this account is that there is no judging of the items that she purchases. No matter how silly or ridiculous or wasteful a dad might think it is; to her, it means the world.

I would try and give her $40 every month to put into her account. She would then use it to buy lunch one or 2 days. Or she would go shopping at Target or ROSS for a couple little items. I do not think it was the actual amount of money that gave her the good feeling; I think it was the idea. It was easy to notice that she was uncomfortable asking for money, pleading her case to try and secure the funds necessary to go somewhere or buy something. This gave her that little bit of freedom to do as she chose and be her own boss again.

My Liz was a very independent person before I met her. She owned her own business and had her own money. After becoming pregnant and developing preeclampsia early on, she could no longer physically work. The days were too long, and she felt sick too often to get anything done. To transition so quickly from independence to dependence is extremely difficult for anyone. No questions asked money is a simple way to restore some of what was lost.

To find the extra $10 per week to give to her, it was simple after I began adding up the little hidden costs throughout my workweek. I eliminated my Red Bull habit and quit supersizing my meals, and there was an extra $10 easy. Truthfully, that is all it comes down to most of the time, merely saving your soft drink money. Also, avoid those small impulse buys, like chewing gum, and an additional $10+ per week will find you.

Gratitude

Forever try and remain in a feeling of gratitude. Be grateful everyday for all that you have. Be grateful for the love of your spouse and family. Be grateful that you have good food to eat and fresh water to drink. There are countless little conveniences that we take for granted that we can all be grateful for. Not only say thank you, both to yourself and out loud, but also make sure that you can feel the feelings of being grateful. When we can truly be grateful for what we already have, we will begin to attract more things to be grateful for into our lives through the Law of Attraction. Wallace Wattles wrote in his book, *The Science of Getting Rich*, back in 1910, that when we are in a good vibration, the universe will align itself with us, and we will begin to attract more good things into our lives.

We are truly grateful that you purchased our book and read through it to the end. It is our sincere hope that this book has been of value to you and that you were able to learn from our experience with preeclampsia. As you can clearly see, this will have an effect on both new parents. It will take a team effort to be successful with each person doing his or her part. You will be happy to know, however, that no matter how bad it gets during the pregnancy, it will get better. And even though your wife or girlfriend may be saying she will never have another child, just as my wife did, that becomes a distant memory after only 6 short months, post-partum.

If you have a success story of your own, we would love for you to share it with us on our website, MyPreeclampsia.com and become the inspiration for hundreds of thousands of women who go through this every year.

We are donating 10% of all profits from this book to help fund preeclampsia research. It is our goal to help with finding a cure for this disease as soon as possible. With 1 out of 10 women suffering with this condition, it is too big of a problem to ignore.

Thank you again for purchasing this book. We love you, and hope to hear of your personal success real soon!

30-Day Meal Plan

All of the advice for the best dietary choices to make while pregnant is important, but sometimes it is difficult to take good information and figure out what you really should be eating. What follows is a meal plan that covers an entire month of good food choices. But don't take my word for it. Dr. Karen Viera, who has her PhD in Biomedical Sciences from the University of Florida College of Medicine created it. She previously led the Kraft Foods cell-based discovery team for health and wellness ingredients. She is on advisory boards for schools and supplement companies. And best of all she has always considered herself a life-long student and teacher of living and healing naturally.

With that said, let me also stress that Dr. Karen Vieira is a Ph.D.-level medical researcher, not a physician. I personally helped my wife overcome preeclampsia and am not a physician. Please consult your primary care physician before beginning any new program of nutrition or dietary supplementation. By consulting your primary care physician, you will have a better opportunity to understand and address your particular symptoms and situation in the most effective ways possible.

Day 1

Breakfast – Egg, spinach, turkey bacon and cheese omelet

Snack – Fat free plain yogurt with honey, crushed flaxseeds and peanuts stirred in

Lunch – Chicken breast, lettuce, tomato, onion and whole wheat bread sandwich

Snack – String cheese and cashew nuts

Dinner – Herb-crusted baked salmon, brown rice and green beans

Dessert – Crushed dried dates mixed with honey and crushed flaxseeds

Day 2

Breakfast – Oatmeal with apple pieces and a small grilled steak

Snack – Trail mix with nuts, flaxseeds and dried fruits

Lunch – Spinach salad with mandarin oranges, mushrooms, almond slices and tuna fish

Snack – Low fat cottage cheese and fruit preserves stirred in

Dinner – Chicken and vegetable kabobs (sweet red peppers, zucchini and red onions)

Dessert – Homemade "Jell-o" made from gelatin powder with apple juice and honey

Day 3

Breakfast – Breakfast quesadilla with eggs, tomato, cheese and tortilla with pineapple

Snack – Orange and strawberries

Lunch – Grilled chicken sandwich and a side salad with ground flaxseeds on top

Snack – Handful of almonds and an apple

Dinner – Mackarel and stir fried vegetables on whole wheat or brown rice pasta

Dessert – Frozen bananas

Day 4

Breakfast – Whole grain cereal with flaxseeds and banana plus a hardboiled egg

Snack – Mango smoothie

Lunch – Grilled chicken Caesar salad with walnuts and low fat dressing

Snack – Cheese cubes and an apple

Dinner – Baked salmon filet, brown rice and green salad with olive oil and vinegar

Dessert – Yogurt parfait with fruit

Day 5

Breakfast – Whole wheat toast with peanut butter and fruit on the side

Snack – Raw carrots, celery, broccoli and cauliflower with veggie dip

Lunch – Egg salad sandwich on whole wheat bread

Snack – Cottage cheese with walnuts and cantaloupe slices

Dinner –BBQ chicken with yellow rice, grilled eggplant and zucchini

Dessert – Warm cherries with ricotta cheese and toasted almonds

Day 6

Breakfast – Egg, mushroom and tomato omelet with melon slices on the side

Snack – Cashew nuts and grapes

Lunch – Natural hot dog on a whole wheat bun

Snack – Hummus with raw veggies and pita chips

Dinner –Tuna fish casserole with whole wheat pasta elbows, black beans and corn

Dessert – Broiled fresh/ frozen mango slices

Day 7

Breakfast – Whole grain cereal with flaxseeds and banana plus cheese cubes

Snack – Strawberry smoothie

Lunch – Crab meat pasta salad with chopped walnuts on top

Snack – Hardboiled egg and an orange

Dinner – Beef stew with whole wheat cous cous and a salad with ground flaxseeds

Dessert – Fruit sorbet

Day 8

Breakfast – Hardboiled eggs, turkey bacon and fruit

Snack – Yogurt with berries and crushed walnuts

Lunch – Fish, cheese, lettuce and tomato burrito

Snack – Whole wheat and flaxseed crackers with Swiss cheese

Dinner – Baked chicken parmesan with brown rice and broccoli

Dessert – Frozen yogurt topped with peanuts

Day 9

Breakfast – Muesli with fruit, nuts and milk

Snack – Celery and peanut butter

Lunch – Chicken and pear on a spinach salad

Snack – Cheddar cheese cubes and an apple

Dinner – Pork and black bean soup with whole wheat and flaxseed crackers

Dessert – Oatmeal raisin cookies

Day 10

Breakfast – Scrambled egg and a bowl of whole grain cereal with ground flaxseeds

Snack – Walnuts and pecans

Lunch – BLT wrap with a side salad

Snack – Veggie sticks and ranch dip

Dinner – Beef and barley soup

Dessert – Dried figs

Day 11

Breakfast – Ham and egg sandwich on whole wheat and flaxseed toast

Snack – Berries and ricotta cheese

Lunch – Tuna fish and cheese quesadilla

Snack – Cherries and cashews

Dinner – Rotisserie chicken with stir fry vegetables over brown rice

Dessert – Fruit salad with whipped topping

Day 12

Breakfast – Turkey bacon and egg melt on a whole wheat English muffin

Snack – Fruit and chopped walnuts stirred into plain fat-free yogurt

Lunch – Salmon filet and baked potato with broccoli, salsa and sour cream

Snack – String cheese and dried apricots

Dinner – Chicken pot pie

Dessert – Gingersnap cookies

Day 13

Breakfast – Egg, whole wheat and flaxseed toast and half a grapefruit

Snack – Can of tuna on whole wheat crackers

Lunch – Beef taco salad topped with lettuce, tomato and onion

Snack – Cheese cubes and an orange

Dinner – Chicken tortilla soup

Dessert – Crystallized ginger and crushed walnuts over vanilla ice cream

Day 14

Breakfast – Scrambled eggs with onion, tomato, green peppers and tuna fish

Snack – Fruit kabobs of pineapple, melon and grapes

Lunch – Turkey burger in whole wheat bun with lettuce, tomato and onion

Snack – Fruit smoothie

Dinner – Grilled salmon, broccoli and couscous

Dessert – Oranges segments topped with cinnamon and brown sugar

Day 15

Breakfast – Eggs Florentine and low-fat sausage

Snack – Handful of dates and apricots with peanuts

Lunch – Tuna salad sandwich on whole wheat and flaxseed bread with lettuce

Snack – Brie with whole wheat crackers and a banana

Dinner – Beef stir fry over wild rice with corn on the cob

Dessert – Banana, peach and milk smoothie

Day 16

Breakfast – Egg, spinach and cheese omelet with turkey bacon

Snack – Fat free yogurt with added fruit and chopped walnuts

Lunch – Turkey breast slices, cheese, lettuce and tomato whole wheat sandwich

Snack – String cheese and mandarin oranges

Dinner – Herb-crusted baked cod, rice pilaf and veggie medley of peas, carrots, corn

Dessert – Cinnamon apples over ice cream

Day 17

Breakfast – Oatmeal with blueberries and a banana

Snack – Ricotta cheese with fruit salad

Lunch – Spinach, onion, tomato, walnuts and grilled chicken breast salad

Snack – Almonds and dried apricots

Dinner – Grilled salmon with grilled vegetables and potato salad

Dessert – Dark chocolate bar

Day 18

Breakfast – Egg, cheese and tortilla quesadilla plus an apple

Snack – Raw veggies with cheese dip

Lunch – Turkey sandwich on whole wheat and flaxseed bread with lettuce and tomato

Snack – Cottage cheese with raspberries and chopped walnuts stirred in

Dinner – Cod fish in tomato sauce with whole wheat pasta and a side salad

Dessert – Frozen yogurt

Day 19

Breakfast – Whole grain cereal with a banana and a hardboiled egg on the side

Snack – Pear and a plum

Lunch – Grilled chicken Caesar salad topped with walnuts

Snack – String cheese and an apple

Dinner – Lemon pepper salmon filet with black beans and rice and green beans

Dessert – Strawberries sprinkled with balsamic vinegar and brown sugar

Day 20

Breakfast – Fried egg with cheese, grilled steak and whole wheat toast

Snack – Seed mix including sunflower, pumpkin, flax and other seeds

Lunch – Egg salad sandwich on whole wheat and flaxseed bread

Snack – Cottage cheese with natural jam and chopped walnuts stirred in

Dinner – BBQ chicken with pasta Alfredo

Dessert – Mango and banana slices topped with melted dark chocolate

Day 21

Breakfast – Egg, mushroom, cheese and tomato omelet with turkey bacon

Snack – Fruit smoothie

Lunch – Natural hot dog in whole wheat bun

Snack – Hummus with pita chips

Dinner – Tuna casserole with whole wheat pasta and a side of corn on the cob

Dessert – Mixed berries topped with grated coconut and whipped cream

Day 22

Breakfast – Whole grain cereal with ground flaxseeds and a banana

Snack – Homemade "Jell-o"- gelatin powder with pineapple juice and honey

Lunch – Crab meat pasta salad topped with crumbled walnuts

Snack – Hardboiled egg and an orange

Dinner – Beef stew with potatoes and carrots included with a side salad

Dessert – Frozen yogurt topped with raspberries and nuts

Day 23

Breakfast – Hardboiled egg, turkey bacon and fruit

Snack – Fat free yogurt with pineapple chunks

Lunch – Chicken, cheese, lettuce, tomato and avocado burrito

Snack – Whole wheat crackers with cheddar cheese

Dinner – Baked salmon with brown rice and stir fry vegetables

Dessert – Plain fat-free yogurt mixed with canned pumpkin puree and honey

Day 24

Breakfast – Oatmeal with apples, cinnamon and maple syrup plus turkey sausage

Snack – Celery and peanut butter

Lunch – Chicken, walnut and pear over a romaine lettuce and tomato salad

Snack – Cheddar cheese cubes and an apple

Dinner – Beef, rice and lentil soup

Desert – Dark chocolate bar

Day 25

Breakfast – Scrambled egg and small bowl of whole grain cereal

Snack – Walnuts, cashews and cheese cubes

Lunch – BLT wrap in whole wheat tortilla

Snack – Vegetables and dip

Dinner – Grilled fish, refried beans, lettuce, tomato and cheese tacos

Dessert – Chocolate-covered cashew nuts

Day 26

Breakfast – Ham, egg and cheese sandwich on whole wheat and flaxseed toast

Snack – Berries and ricotta cheese

Lunch – Grilled chicken sandwich and coleslaw

Snack – Almonds and macadamias with a plum

Dinner – Spinach salad with corn, cheese, ground flaxseed and sliced grilled steak

Dessert – Oatmeal raisin cookies

Day 27

Breakfast – Turkey bacon, egg and cheese melt on whole wheat French bread

Snack – Fruit and honey stirred into fat-free plain yogurt

Lunch – Grilled chicken breast and baked potato with sour cream and turkey bacon

Snack – Low fat cottage cheese with berries and chopped walnuts

Dinner – Turkey meatloaf with mashed red potatoes and Brussels sprouts

Dessert – Peach cobbler made with whole grain flour

Day 28

Breakfast – Boiled egg, sausage, whole wheat and flaxseed toast and half a grapefruit

Snack – Pistachios and strawberries

Lunch – Chicken, noodle and vegetable soup with whole grain pasta

Snack – Cheese stick and an orange

Dinner – Curried salmon with brown rice and steamed cabbage

Dessert – Fruit salad

Day 29

Breakfast – Scrambled eggs with onion, tomato, green peppers and turkey bacon

Snack – Nectarine and cheese cubes

Lunch – Turkey burger on whole wheat and flaxseed bread with lettuce and tomato

Snack – Fruit smoothie

Dinner – Grilled tuna filet, whole wheat pasta and broccoli

Dessert – Fat-free yogurt and cream cheese blended and topped with berries

Day 30

Breakfast – Oatmeal with blueberries and ground flaxseeds plus a hardboiled egg

Snack – Whole wheat pita chips with hummus

Lunch – Tuna salad and cheese whole wheat sandwich

Snack – Peanuts, walnuts and a banana

Dinner – Grilled pork chop and grilled potatoes with cucumber salad

Dessert – Whole wheat fruit cake

Conclusion

The meal guide is merely that—a guide. Swap things out so you include your favorite fish, lean meats, cheeses, whole grains, nuts and seeds. And use whatever fruits and vegetables are in season at the time. Also, spice everything up to suit your taste buds using fresh herbs whenever possible. Insert your own drinks, making sure to get lots of water and low-fat milk, with some unsweetened fruit juices for added variety.

As you make substitutions to please your tastes, make sure to eat plenty of salmon, flaxseeds and walnuts to get your omega-3s. Also eat several dairy products like cheese, yogurt and cottage cheese to get enough calcium. Spinach is another good source of calcium. Eat plenty of fruits, vegetables and whole grains in order to get high levels of fiber. Make sure to include protein with every meal or snack, like meat, fish, egg, cheese or nuts in order to get 80 grams or more of protein daily.

While fresh fruits and vegetables are good, frozen ones have the same levels of nutrients or even more sometimes since they are frozen quickly after being picked. So don't be limited to only the fruits and vegetables that are in season. While most canned foods are not healthy, some canned foods are actually not bad. A few good ones that you can use are tuna fish in water, sardines in water and tomato paste.

When shopping, try to stick to the perimeter of the supermarket, since that is where the majority of healthy foods are. The sides and back of the supermarket have meats, fish, fruits, vegetables and fresh breads. Only go down the aisles for a few healthy items like oats, whole grain cereal, canned fish, natural jam, dried fruits, nuts and seeds.

As with most other things in life, planning will go a long way as you create a successful experience. Taking the time to plan a weekly menu, create a shopping list and shopping for only what is on your list can help you avoid last minute bad decisions. If every meal is planned in advance, there will be no worrying about what to fix for dinner which will reduce the number of times poor choices are made. And by planning the grocery shopping around the menu it will be easier to have the necessary ingredients available. Having the list while in the grocery store will also keep you from impulse purchasing. Impulse buys are usually poor choices and have low nutritional value.

By not buying junk foods, you have no choice but to eat healthy meals and snacks. So make it a point to stock your home, car, purse and desk drawer with healthy snacks and on-the-go meals. That way you won't fall into the trap of eating anything that can cause or worsen preeclampsia.

When cooking, it is important to avoid using large quantities of oil or butter. Instead buy organic butter or coconut oil and use them sparingly in your cooking. Also buy olive oil and use that as a dressing on your salads. By choosing low fat meats and cooking them with very little oil, you will drastically reduce your intake of bad fats which can cause preeclampsia.

It is very important to make conscious choices, both for your health and the health of your unborn child. Both of you are depending on the choices that you make.

Preeclampsia is a dangerous condition for pregnant women and their babies. Follow your doctor's advice and the information in this guide to help reduce the risk of developing this potentially fatal disease. Aim to eat foods high in fiber, protein, calcium, magnesium and vitamins, to ensure that both you and your baby will be healthy.

References

1. Helewa ME, Burrows RF, Smith J, Williams K, Brain P, Rabkin SW: Report of the Canadian Hypertension Society Consensus Conference: 1. Definitions, evaluation and classification of hypertensive disorders in pregnancy. *CMAJ.* 1997;157(6):715-725.

2. Report of the National High Blood Pressure Education Program Working Group on High Blood Pressure in Pregnancy. *Am J Obstet Gynecol.* 2000;183(1):S1-S22.

3. Duley L: The global impact of preeclampsia and eclampsia. *Semin Perinatol.* 2009;33(3):130-137.

4. Khan KS, Wojdyla D, Say L, Gulmezoglu AM, Van Look PF: WHO analysis of causes of maternal death: a systematic review. *Lancet.* 2006;367(9516):1066-1074.

5. Meis PJ, Goldenberg RL, Mercer BM, et al.: The preterm prediction study: risk factors for indicated preterm births. Maternal-Fetal Medicine Units Network of the National Institute of Child Health and Human Development. *Am J Obstet Gynecol.* 1998;178(3):562-567.

6. Whitfield MF, Grunau RV, Holsti L: Extremely premature (< or = 800 g) schoolchildren: multiple areas of hidden disability. *Arch Dis Child Fetal Neonatal Ed.* 1997;77(2):F85-90.

7. Frederick IO, Williams MA, Dashow E, Kestin M, Zhang C, Leisenring WM: Dietary fiber, potassium, magnesium and calcium in relation to the risk of preeclampsia. *J Reprod Med.* 2005;50(5):332-344.

8. Qiu C, Coughlin KB, Frederick IO, Sorensen TK, Williams MA: Dietary fiber intake in early pregnancy and risk of subsequent preeclampsia. *Am J Hypertens.* 2008;21(8):903-909.

9. Rosing U, Samsioe G, Olund A, Johansson B, Kallner A: Serum levels of apolipoprotein A-I, A-II and HDL-cholesterol in second half of normal pregnancy and in pregnancy complicated by preeclampsia. *Horm Metab Res.* 1989;21(7):376-382.

10. Kaaja R, Tikkanen MJ, Viinikka L, Ylikorkala O: Serum lipoproteins, insulin, and urinary prostanoid metabolites in normal and hypertensive pregnant women. *Obstet Gynecol.* 1995;85(3):353-356.

11. Robinson NJ, Minchell LJ, Myers JE, Hubel CA, Crocker IP: A potential role for free fatty acids in the pathogenesis of preeclampsia. *J Hypertens.* 2009;27(6):1293-1302.

12. Kokia E, Barkai G, Reichman B, Segal P, Goldman B, Mashiach S: Maternal serum lipid profile in pregnancies complicated by hypertensive disorders. *J Perinat Med.* 1990;18(6):473-478.

13. Potter JM, Nestel PJ: The hyperlipidemia of pregnancy in normal and complicated pregnancies. *Am J Obstet Gynecol.* 1979;133(2):165-170.

14. Sattar N, Bendomir A, Berry C, Shepherd J, Greer IA, Packard CJ: Lipoprotein subfraction concentrations in preeclampsia: pathogenic parallels to atherosclerosis. *Obstet Gynecol.* 1997;89(3):403-408.

15. Qiu C, Sanchez SE, Larrabure G, David R, Bralley JA, Williams MA: Erythrocyte omega-3 and omega-6 polyunsaturated fatty acids and preeclampsia risk in Peruvian women. *Arch Gynecol Obstet.* 2006;274(2):97-103.

16. Wang Y, Walsh SW, Kay HH: Placental tissue levels of nonesterified polyunsaturated fatty acids in normal and preeclamptic pregnancies. *Hypertens Pregnancy.* 2005;24(3):235-245.

17. Al MD, von Houwelingen AC, Hasaart TH, Hornstra G: The relationship between the essential fatty acid status of mother and child and the occurrence of pregnancy-induced hypertension. Intermediate results of a prospective longitudinal study. *World Rev Nutr Diet.* 1994;76:110-113.

18. Al MD, van Houwelingen AC, Badart-Smook A, Hasaart TH, Roumen FJ, Hornstra G: The essential fatty acid status of mother and child in pregnancy-induced hypertension: a prospective longitudinal study. *Am J Obstet Gynecol.* 1995;172(5):1605-1614.

19. Williams MA, Zingheim RW, King IB, Zebelman AM: Omega-3 fatty acids in maternal erythrocytes and risk of preeclampsia. *Epidemiology.* 1995;6(3):232-237.

20. Wang YP, Kay HH, Killam AP: Decreased levels of polyunsaturated fatty acids in preeclampsia. *Am J Obstet Gynecol.* 1991;164(3):812-818.

21. Olsen SF, Secher NJ, Tabor A, Weber T, Walker JJ, Gluud C: Randomised clinical trials of fish oil supplementation in high risk pregnancies. Fish Oil Trials In Pregnancy (FOTIP) Team. *BJOG.* 2000;107(3):382-395.

22. Onwude JL, Lilford RJ, Hjartardottir H, Staines A, Tuffnell D: A randomised double blind placebo controlled trial of fish oil in high risk pregnancy. *Br J Obstet Gynaecol.* 1995;102(2):95-100.

23. Salvig JD, Olsen SF, Secher NJ: Effects of fish oil supplementation in late pregnancy on blood pressure: a randomised controlled trial. *Br J Obstet Gynaecol.* 1996;103(6):529-533.

24. Hofmeyr GJ, Lawrie TA, Atallah AN, Duley L: Calcium supplementation during pregnancy for preventing hypertensive disorders and related problems. *Cochrane Database Syst Rev.* 2010;8:CD001059.

25. Herrera JA, Shahabuddin AK, Ersheng G, Wei Y, Garcia RG, Lopez-Jaramillo P: Calcium plus linoleic acid therapy for pregnancy-induced hypertension. *Int J Gynaecol Obstet.* 2005;91(3):221-227.

26. Duley L, Henderson-Smart D: Reduced salt intake compared to normal dietary salt, or high intake, in pregnancy. *Cochrane Database Syst Rev.* 2000(2):CD001687.

27. Nabeshima K: [Effect of salt restriction on preeclampsia]. *Nippon Jinzo Gakkai Shi.* 1994;36(3):227-232.

28. van der Maten GD: Low sodium diet in pregnancy: effects on maternal nutritional status. *Eur J Obstet Gynecol Reprod Biol.* 1995;61(1):63-64.

29. van der Maten GD, van Raaij JM, Visman L, et al.: Low-sodium diet in pregnancy: effects on blood pressure and maternal nutritional status. *Br J Nutr.* 1997;77(5):703-720.

30. Llurba E, Gratacos E, Martin-Gallan P, Cabero L, Dominguez C: A comprehensive study of oxidative stress and antioxidant status in preeclampsia and normal pregnancy. *Free Radic Biol Med.* 2004;37(4):557-570.

31. Bowen RS, Mars M, Chuturgoon AA, Dutton MF, Moodley J: The response of the dietary anti-oxidants vitamin E and vitamin C to oxidative stress in preeclampsia. *J Obstet Gynaecol.* 1998;18(1):9-13.

32. Qiu C, Phung TT, Vadachkoria S, Muy-Rivera M, Sanchez SE, Williams MA: Oxidized low-density lipoprotein (Oxidized LDL) and the risk of preeclampsia. *Physiol Res.* 2006;55(5):491-500.

33. Sagol S, Ozkinay E, Ozsener S: Impaired antioxidant activity in women with preeclampsia. *Int J Gynaecol Obstet.* 1999;64(2):121-127.

34. Zhang C, Williams MA, King IB, et al.: Vitamin C and the risk of preeclampsia--results from dietary questionnaire and plasma assay. *Epidemiology.* 2002;13(4):409-416.

35. Mikhail MS, Anyaegbunam A, Garfinkel D, Palan PR, Basu J, Romney SL: Preeclampsia and antioxidant nutrients: decreased plasma levels of reduced ascorbic acid, alpha-tocopherol, and beta-carotene in women with preeclampsia. *Am J Obstet Gynecol.* 1994;171(1):150-157.

36. Kharb S: Vitamin E and C in preeclampsia. *Eur J Obstet Gynecol Reprod Biol.* 2000;93(1):37-39.

37. Kharb S, Gulati N, Singh V, Singh GP: Lipid peroxidation and vitamin E levels in preeclampsia. *Gynecol Obstet Invest.* 1998;46(4):238-240.

38. Madazli R, Benian A, Gumustas K, Uzun H, Ocak V, Aksu F: Lipid peroxidation and antioxidants in preeclampsia. *Eur J Obstet Gynecol Reprod Biol.* 1999;85(2):205-208.

39. Chappell LC, Seed PT, Briley AL, et al.: Effect of antioxidants on the occurrence of preeclampsia in women at increased risk: a randomised trial. *Lancet.* 1999;354(9181):810-816.

40. Ziari SA, Mireles VL, Cantu CG, et al.: Serum vitamin A, vitamin E, and beta-carotene levels in preeclamptic women in northern nigeria. *Am J Perinatol.* 1996;13(5):287-291.

41. Jendryczko A, Drozdz M: Plasma retinol, beta-carotene and vitamin E levels in relation to the future risk of preeclampsia. *Zentralbl Gynakol.* 1989;111(16):1121-1123.

42. Williams MA, Woelk GB, King IB, Jenkins L, Mahomed K: Plasma carotenoids, retinol, tocopherols, and lipoproteins in preeclamptic and normotensive pregnant Zimbabwean women. *Am J Hypertens.* 2003;16(8):665-672.

43. Koskinen T, Valtonen P, Lehtovaara I, Tuimala R: Amniotic fluid retinol concentrations in late pregnancy. *Biol Neonate.* 1986;49(2):81-84.

44. Hernandez-Diaz S, Werler MM, Louik C, Mitchell AA: Risk of gestational hypertension in relation to folic acid supplementation during pregnancy. *Am J Epidemiol.* 2002;156(9):806-812.

45. Wen SW, Chen XK, Rodger M, et al.: Folic acid supplementation in early second trimester and the risk of preeclampsia. *Am J Obstet Gynecol.* 2008;198(1):45 e41-47.

46. Ray JG, Mamdani MM: Association between folic acid food fortification and hypertension or preeclampsia in pregnancy. *Arch Intern Med.* 2002;162(15):1776-1777.

47. Haugen M, Brantsaeter AL, Trogstad L, et al.: Vitamin D supplementation and reduced risk of preeclampsia in nulliparous women. *Epidemiology.* 2009;20(5):720-726.
48. Which anticonvulsant for women with eclampsia? Evidence from the Collaborative Eclampsia Trial. *Lancet.* 1995;345(8963):1455-1463.
49. Conradt A, Weidinger H, Algayer H: [The significance of betamimetics and magnesium for the outcome of pregnancy: II. The role of magnesium in the development of gestosis and fetal hypotrophy]. *Z Geburtshilfe Perinatol.* 1983;187(6):264-272.
50. Jain S, Sharma P, Kulshreshtha S, Mohan G, Singh S: The role of calcium, magnesium, and zinc in preeclampsia. *Biol Trace Elem Res.* 2010;133(2):162-170.

CPSIA information can be obtained at www.ICGtesting.com
Printed in the USA
LVOW082058180613

339167LV00002B/581/P

9 780557 557097